I0838980

The History of

Dissociative Identity Disorder (DID)

By

Dr. Jack Grenan, PhD

Dedication

This Guide is dedicated to those who have loved and supported me throughout this project as well as many of life's trials and tribulations; My loving wife Nancy, my daughters Katie and Kelly and my sons Jimmy & Shaun, my awesome grandchildren and my grandparents Katherine and Bill Mackesy, who gave me love and hope.

Acknowledgement

I would like to acknowledge the following people: Dr. Carroll and Dr. Borrelli for their guidance and assistance in completing this thesis; Dr. Jay Zarowitz of Muskegon Community College for his kindness and support; and Dr. Jansma who showed me, by example and kindness, how to be a good therapist. Last and most of all, my wife Nancy for typing a great portion of this thesis and for putting up with our home full of the books and papers I used to complete this research.

Abstract

The literature review examined the history of Dissociation Identity Disorder (DID) previously referred to as Multiple Personality Disorder (MPD). The review dealt with literature from ancient Egyptian times through 1994 when the American Psychological Association (APA) officially changed the term from MPD to DID to the present. The historical review of this mental coping mechanism in the face of trauma began with the ancient Egyptians when some gods were composed of the essence of multiple creatures to form one god. These ancient cultures set a foundation that western culture used to assist in the creation of the field of psychology. The review continues into the late eighteen-hundreds, as Freud, Charcot, Janet and others not only diagnose a condition of hysteria but initiate treatment. The review continued through the combat trauma war in the twentieth century in which post-traumatic stress was found to lead to DID. From the nineteen-fifties to the nineteen-nineties, several well-publicized cases of MPD were reviewed. The final result is one document that provides therapists and lay-persons alike with the history of dissociation and MPD that assists in their understanding of the condition.

CHAPTER 1: INTRODUCTION TO THE LITERATURE REVIEW

Introduction

The search for information concerning the history of Dissociative Identity Disorder (DID), formally Multiple Personality Disorder (MPD), should begin with the earliest known records of man. Whether these records are ancient writings to pass on to future generations or written documents such as the Egyptian Book of the Dead, this was where the search for any clues of behavior that mirrors that of Dissociation began. One would expect that if dissociative behavior is a reaction of the mind to protect the self when facing severe trauma that a researcher would find some evidence of this behavior in ancient texts and documents that describe human behavior under traumatic conditions.

Based on man's history of war, poor health conditions, and violent, uncivilized societies, a researcher would expect to find descriptions of traumatic situations that lead to dissociative behavior. While the review of literature from various ancient times may or may not be fruitful in finding evidence of dissociative behavior, it is important to search these eras to be thorough in the attempt to write as complete a history of Dissociative Identity Disorder as possible.

One benefit of this approach was the accumulation of historical evidence of the existence of dissociation in humans that may result in a better understanding of how and why the mind dissociates. It is believed that additional information will result in a better understanding of the phenomena leading to better treatment for those who suffer from the condition.

Statement of the Problem

Dissociative Identity Disorder is a coping mechanism that eventually leads the victim of severe trauma to dysfunction. To further enhance the therapist's ability to assist these unfortunate victims who, unconsciously, resort to DID to survive. It is important that a better understanding of the historical aspects of dissociatives is established to add to the understanding of this coping behavior.

Currently, there is disagreement among therapists and academics on whether or not dissociative identity disorder actually exists. Some believe that it is a true condition needing treatment, while some believe that dissociative behavior is created by a therapist. While this disagreement will most likely never be resolved, some respectable researchers such as Ross (1989), one of the leading proponents of the DID theory, believes that the percentage of people suffering from Dissociative Identity Disorder is one to two percent of the United States population (Ross, 1989). Based on the lower estimate of one per cent of a population of 293 million United States citizens, this would extrapolate to nearly three million cases of DID (CIA, 2004). These cases, in addition to the therapist's case reports, validate the need to learn more about the history of DID.

What Is Dissociative Identity Disorder?

Dissociation is the disconnection of various thoughts, memories and emotions from the conscious self that are usually connected. This can result in behavioral dysfunction as the individual attempts to connect to others in their personal world of work and family. The person is often unaware of some self-defeating behaviors that previously worked at a younger age but is

detrimental as an adult. This usually leads
to problems in their work and personal
relationships.

The conscious self is the sum total of a
person's genetic components, memories,
experiences and personality, that combine to
create the body of information that the
individual is aware of and can retrieve from
their conscious memory.

To dissociate means to disconnect from
the reality of the present. Identity is
defined as who you are, which is composed of
an individual's genetics, feelings, memories,
and experiences that combine to create a
unique individual, or the self. A person's
identity includes the conscious and
unconscious self. Disorder means that the

system or parts of the self or personality are not working or interacting as they are designed to interact, in order for the true self to connect to the outer world (Masterson, 1990).

According to Masterson (1990), persons who have a behavior disorder are, "unable to accomplish the task of finding a fit with their environment and are compelled to resort to self-destructive behavior patterns – evidence of a false self that protect them from feeling bad at the cost of a meaningful and fulfilling life. The false self, unable to experiment, induces lack of self-esteem as the person has to settle for rigid, destructive behavior that avoids life's challenges but leads to feelings of failure,

lost hopes and unfulfilled dreams and
despair" Masterson, 1990,p.viii). Although
there are many other definitions, Masterson's
definition is accurate, simple, and to the
point.

Section 300.14 of Diagnostic
Statistical Disorder IV (DSM IV) Manual lists
the four criteria for a diagnosis of DID:
The presence of two or more distinct
identities or personality states (each with
its own relatively enduring pattern of
perceiving, relating to, and thinking about
the environment and self).

A. At least two identities or personality
   states recurrently taking control of the
   person's behavior.

B. Inability to recall important personal

information that is too extensive to be explained by ordinary forgetfulness.

C. The disturbance is not due to direct physiological effects of a substance (e.g. blackouts or chaotic behavior during alcohol intoxication) or a general medical condition (e.g. complex seizures). Note: In children, the symptoms are not attributed to imaginary playmates or other fantasy play (American Psychiatric Association, 2000, p529).

The current controversy concerning Dissociative Identity Disorder appears to have made the transition from the need to prove that it exists to the position of what could be learned about DID to better diagnose

and treat this condition. This is a much more
fruitful position for researchers and clients
alike. The purpose of conducting a literature
review of the history of MPD/DID is to update
and consolidate the various sources of
information regarding this coping behavior.

Background to the Problem

There has been ongoing discussion and
disagreement among psychologists,
psychiatrists, physicians and others, not
only about Dissociative Identity Disorder
(DID) (previously referred to as Multiple
Personality Disorder or MPD), but about its
very existence. Since the days of Freud,
Charcot and Janet, the descriptions of
hysterical episodes initiated curiosity and

research into these behaviors.

This paper takes the position that Dissociative Identity Disorder not only exists but is an ingenious, effective, and sane coping mechanism of the human mind in response to the most insane, unimaginable experiences that some unfortunate human beings encounter. Yet, this same coping mechanism, dissociation, which is created for the survival of the self, later becomes a destructive barrier to the growth and stability of the self. These dissociative initiated coping strategies that protect the self in reaction to childhood trauma become ineffective as the demands of adult life require more and different coping strategies. This, in part, is why a diagnosis of

Dissociative Identity Disorder is, often not confirmed until the victim of trauma is an adult. Coping behavior that was successful or tolerated at earlier ages becomes unsuccessful and even detrimental in adult situations such as the workplace and/or adult personal relationships.

Most people exhibiting dissociative behavior seek treatment meet with several therapists until a diagnosis of DID is correctly evaluated. This is due, in part, to the masking of the disorder by the client and, in some cases, a lack of training in diagnosing this condition by therapists.

Today, there is an abundance of literature on the subjects of personality, multiple personality, and dissociation.

Various abstracts, selected texts and articles were read in search of historical data. The focus of this literature review is to obtain additional information about the history of DID and add it to the current pool of knowledge in one document.

The literature review examined the history of Dissociation dating back to the ancient writings of the Egyptians, Greeks, and Romans, and continued through the Middle Ages. It continued with the introduction of hypnosis and the work of Freud, Janet, Charcot and others with hysterical patients. The last time period was from World War I to the present.

This historical study of dissociation included written documentation of the diagnosis and treatment of soldiers from World War I, World War II, the Korean and Vietnam Wars, who suffered from Post-Traumatic Stress Disorder and provided evidence of Dissociative Behavior. Numerous combat veterans exhibited symptoms of DID but these symptoms were often ignored or dismissed. While the number of diagnosed and documented cases of DID have increased, skepticism has also increased. This makes the need for and importance of further research of DID more important than ever for clients and therapists alike.

Purpose of the Study

One objective of this critical review was to locate, expand, summarize, and add knowledge to the current research concerning MPD and DID. Presently, those seeking a comprehensive reference document of the history and evolution of the diagnosis and treatment of DID are required to spend countless hours perusing through various resources. Another goal of this thesis was to provide the reader with one document that consolidates many of the major historical accounts of and theories for DID. This will result in assisting therapists and laypersons alike to become, better informed concerning DID which will assist them in understanding the condition and developing treatment plans.

Methodology for Historical Review

The selection of articles and books to

review relative to Dissociation is as follows:

1. Various professional books and historical descriptions by philosophers, practicing doctors, psychologists, therapists and other sources were reviewed and selected based on their relevance to the topic.

1. The Grand Valley State University Library was accessed along with various professional journals, texts, and other sources.

The review is divided into four sections- ancient and medieval times, western civilization from medieval times to pre-World War I, World War I to the Gulf War, and case studies in America since the first reported case of Multiple Personality Disorder, in

1906, to the present.

The era of Freud, Charcot, Breuer and others that begins with the famous case study of Anna O. to the numerous post-World War I case descriptions of Post-Traumatic Stress Disorder, were closely analyzed. The cases of hospitalized soldiers with severe emotional distress, were reviewed in search of symptoms and behavior that may mirror behavior described today as Dissociative Identity Disorder.

Research Questions

1. Is there a history of documented cases that contain evidence of Dissociative Identity Disorder?

2. When was the idea of Multiple

Personality Disorder as a coping behavior first put forth in the field of psychology?

3. How was the behavior that today is diagnosed as Dissociative Identity Disorder been documented in the past?

4. Specifically, what is the history of Multiple Personality Disorder/Dissociative Identity Disorder in the United States?

Assumptions, Delimitations and Limitations

The initial assumption is that Dissociative Identity Disorder exists, it can be treated, and integration is a useful goal of treatment but not always desirable.

The research review was limited based on

the limited ability to review unlimited
texts, articles and documents. Most of the
texts that, were reviewed were written in
English and a few were written in French or
German. The Grand Valley State University
library was used to research various sources
of information. The worldwide internet
expanded the search for the most current
literature.

Identification of the Variables

To be Examined

The focus of this literature review was
historical information that may describe
various behaviors that identify and/or
diagnose origins of dissociation. The

variables included genetic, biological,
psychological and environmental factors that
one may expect to be consistent over time to
identify the same condition.

Integration of the Literature Review into the Existing

Pool of Knowledge Concerning Dissociation

The goal was to create a document that gives the reader information that provides an understanding of dissociation's historical roots. The net result of the research is a historical, practical and credible resource document to help therapists, parents, clients and others better understand Dissociative Identity Disorder.

While the goals and parameters of the

literature review are defined in Chapter One, Chapter Two contains the relevant literature collected from thousands of documents that may result in a better understanding of the history of Multiple Personality Disorder and Dissociative Identity Disorder. The literature review in Chapter Two offers of DID. This search begins in ancient times in Egypt and continues with a review of Greek literature into medieval times. Due to the lack of written documentation from these eras, the majority of the literature review is from the late eighteen-hundreds to the present.

Hypnosis and World War I are strongly tied to the history of Multiple Personality Disorder and Dissociative Identity Disorder are reviewed in great detail in this paper. Hypnosis evolved into a tool that is widely used to treat personality disorders and the case studies from World War I contributed greatly to documenting the connection between trauma and dissociative coping behavior.

The last section of Chapter Two looks at the education of the American public about Multiple Personality Disorder and Dissociative Identity Disorder. The research shows that a combination of professional research, combined with the influence of multi-media, resulted in how many Americans learned about these mental illnesses. Understanding DID is an ongoing process for professionals and laypeople alike who have added the internet to the various sources in

the search for answers to better understand
human behavior.

Chapter Three summarizes the findings of
the literature review, provides
recommendations for future research, and
states the social implications of the results
of this research. Also, the four research
questions are answered based on the research
findings.

Definition of Terms

ALTER-IDENTITY—A part of the self that splits
from the main self as a result of
Dissociation.

AMNESIA— Inability to remember events, a loss
of the ability to remember.

BLACKOUT—Occurs when one of the dissociative

parts takes over and there is no memory of that time period.

DISSOCIATE—When the mind is not aware of reality in the present. When this occurs, a separate part of the self replaces the previously established main self.

DISSOCIATION—The condition when the mind dissociates (see above) consistently over time resulting in control of the self by a personality other than the main self.

DISSOCIATIVE—An adjective that describes when a person's personality splinters into several selves in order to protect the central self from traumatic memories.

DISSOCIATIVE IDENTITY DISORDER (DID)—The term in DSM-IV that replaces the diagnostic term MPD.

HOST—The personality and behavior that is most often present in a dissociative person.

IDENTITY—The personality or part that is present at any given time.

INTEGRATION—The healing process that occurs when all of the separate selves accept each other's existence and become unified under the central self or identity.

MULTIPLE—A person with more than oneself or identity. **MULTIPLE PERSONALITY DISORDER (MPD)**—Former term replaced by DID.

PERPETRATOR—A person who causes harm to another; The harm may be physical or mental.

PERSONALITY—The composite of a person's pattern of thoughts, feelings, and behaviors that describes their unique identity.

PRESENT—To be aware of the present/reality.

SPLIT—To develop another self by dissociating.

SURVIVOR—A person who has experienced severe trauma yet is alive and is not overcome by that trauma.

SWITCH—When the mind changes from one self to another.

SYSTEM—The complete group of all the parts that alternate in control of the self.

TRIGGER— A cue that causes a change in the identity in charge or a forgotten memory that is remembered and results in a change of identity (Sidran, 2002 pp. 1-4).

CHAPTER 2: LITERATURE REVIEW

Ancient Historical Writings

Among the various texts reviewed was literature that had previously been overlooked. These ancient documents and other sources provided descriptions of behavior very similar to today's descriptions of dissociative behavior. There are currently thousands of articles and books from which to select that deal with material relative to MPD and DID. The Internet has dramatically changed how information is distributed and allows anyone to post information in the public domain. The literature review began by seeking clues from ancient documents at a time when only a privileged few were allowed an education, and written communication was rare. This was the era of the Egyptians, the time of the Pharaohs.

Among the hieroglyphics that have been translated into English was the Egyptian Book of the Dead. This document was selected for review because of its insights into Egyptian culture and philosophy, which leads to greater insight into dissociative behavior.

The Egyptian Book of the Dead is one of the earliest records of early civilizations (Budge, 1895). In addition to reading this text, there is the Papyrus of Ani, written between BC 1500 and 1400 (Budge, 1895), that explains much of the writings from The Book of the Dead. These documents are of special significance to the history of Dissociation, not only because they are two of the oldest historical documents known, but because they document the influence of religion upon our ancestor's views of the concept of duality of the self. For example, a creature could possess the strength of a lion and wisdom of an eagle. This would result in a new creature composed of the best attributes of both. As is the case with Dissociation, these ancient Egyptian beliefs showed an acceptance of the concept of duality or plurality of the self (Budge, 1895).

In 1895, E.A. Wallis Budge, the keeper responsible for the maintenance of Assyrian and Egyptian Antiquities in an Egyptian museum in Cairo, interpreted of The Book of the Dead and The Papyrus of Ani increasing the availability of these remarkable documents.

The Egyptian Book of the Dead took rituals and incantations that were previously reserved only for the select in Egyptian society and provided other Egyptians of lower castes a document to guide their spirited behavior. The body, mind, and spiritual world combine to oversee the will and fate of man during the time of a powerful man named Ani. Ani was Chancellor of the Ecclesiastical revenue and endowments of Abyclos and Thebes. This document is regarded as a typical funeral book of Ani's time (Budge, 1895).

Among the gods described in the Book of the Dead is Ammit, the eater of the dead.

Interestingly, this creature is a tri-formed monster, part crocodile, part lion, and part hippopotamus (Budge, 1895). In addition to the god being drawn as one god composed of three different animals, Ammit is pictured with a scale. On one plate is a heart and on the other plate is a feather. An Egyptian's life events would be weighed to decide their fate after death.

These passages indicate that ancient Egyptian religious beliefs accepted that their god's identity could be the result of the combination the attributes of two separate gods and this is a central belief in understanding Dissociation. These different parts, each with a unique role, combine with other parts of other creatures to form a new embodiment that is a composite of the three. This is similar to the basic understanding of dissociation today that a person can have several distinct selves in one person. This is not a claim that the Book of the Dead describes Dissociation. However, from the time of the Egyptians, there are many other cultures with a similar belief that gods, and at times people, are composed of different beings that result in unusual behaviors by those inhabited by these spirits (Budge, 1895).

The future of the souls is described in The Book of What Is In the Tuat, that was found in various tombs and coffins of the eighteenth Egyptian Dynasty and following dynasties (Budge, 1895). In this book, the entrance to the underworld is depicted as guarded by a serpent on four legs with a human head. These religious views showed a belief that the physical and moral being are separate, yet combine to decide the fate of men. These ancient texts and religious beliefs may be interpreted as evidence that humans were perceived as multi-faceted beings that were the sum of three parts: the physical, mental, and spiritual (Budge, 1895).

According to Budge, the key beliefs of the Egyptian's religion remained unchanged until the mid-to-first century AD. At this time, a sect in Egypt called the Copts incorporated many of the older beliefs with the new Christian views (History of the

Copts, 2004). These included various superstitious and mythological beliefs and traditions of ancient Egypt. One example is the practice of burying a person with food and other items to be used in the next life (History of the Copts, 2004).

Just as the ancient Egyptians believed in the duality of the self, that a person is more than a body but is also composed of a mind and spirit, so too did many pagans and early Christians. The followers of these religions also believed that a person could be possessed or inhabited by another evil soul who would take over the person's body and mind (History of the Copts, 2004).

Many of these stories tell of the spiritual transformation of a person that results in behaviors very out of character due to this possession. These stories contain similarities to modern day behaviors observed in people diagnosed as Dissociative. Some examples of these behavior changes include, not remembering their actions, a change from usual calm behavior to very aggressive behavior, and even speaking in different voices.

The search for documentation of Dissociative behavior in Greek culture is interesting but difficult due to the necessity of finding translations. In reading many of the texts by the Greek philosophers, one learns more about the Greek contributions that influenced the evolution of today's philosophy, medicine and psychology rather than learn about Dissociative behavior.

Some of these philosophers and their contributions include Pythagoras of Samos, who sought to prove that there is order in the universe. "There is an unknowable body (the world) that each being perceives subjectivity according to their own perceptions" (Guinard, 2003 p.2). This concept foreshadows the modern belief of some therapists that a person's perception, even if containing fantasy, is that person's reality. Such is the belief of a person with a Dissociative personality.

Empedocles of Agrigentun contributed the idea that, "philia (love) and neihos (hate) are inherent in all things "(p.3). This mirrors the duality found in the Egyptian beliefs. These emotions were said to exist in four elements; earth, fire, air, and water, which were deemed to control the earth (Guinard, 2003). This belief is consistent with the Egyptian belief of good versus evil. The belief of good versus evil is a very basic concept that exists in most cultures, and this concept is important in understanding how Dissociation affects a person. Some of the selves in a Dissociative are seen as a negative or evil influence, while others are seen as a positive or good influence. This separation of selves and good versus evil is important for a therapist to investigate in order to assist the Dissociative client.

The constant battle for survival and existence, seen as a battle of good versus evil, is consistent in all of the literature reviewed. In Egyptian, Roman, or Greek philosophy, the belief was that man is in an ongoing struggle between good and evil. This idea is central in the descriptions of possessions by the devil, demons and other entities. Nietzsche (1891) wrote Zarathustra, in this description of man's struggle to find his purpose he describes, " The great cry of distress: it was a strange, complex cry, and sounded like a cry of a single voice. Each of these men has kept their point of view, a human one, far too human in Zarathustra's opinion, over which has risen -even more than antagonism of Good and Evil—psycho-social-personality, necessarily inscribed in the stars as Paracelsus announced in his Astronomia magma. Although they stand isolated in their madness, the superior men remain united by the close relationship that each has with their common product: the absurd cry, of distress which materializes unbeknownst to any of them "(Guinard, 2003, p.6). It is important to understand this aspect of Nietz dissociation because each of the parts of a dissociative person plays a role that is positive or negative or as some see good versus evil.

The ancients sought order and reason to explain the ethereal and corporal world. A supposition of cause and effect, known as the scientific approach, is seen as the best process to understand behavior and the world around us.

A review of ancient literature suggesting beliefs in dissociating experiences would be incomplete without a review of the philosopher and teacher Plato. Plato's teachings were spread worldwide, and accepted by many leading philosophers and educators who have had an impact on the beliefs of Western Civilization. Plato discusses the duality of human beings as the relationship of the body and mind. In his work, the Phraedus, he wrote, "We are enshrined in the living tomb which we carry about, imprisoned in the body as an oyster in a shell" (Plato, 1957, p.32). This is an accurate description of the feelings of some

Dissociatives, who disclose in therapy that
he/she feels a lack of control due to the
uncertainty as to which self is in control at
any given time.

In some post-A.D. cultures, demons,
witches, and/or ghosts were believed to have
the ability to possess a human body. There
were specific ceremonies designed to free the
possessed such as voodoo rituals and
Christian exorcisms. While some relate
possession as possible proof of Dissociation,
there is little proof of this in the reviewed
literature.

In Medieval Europe, the Catholic Church and
State were closely intertwined. The State,
usually a Feudal Lord, used the beliefs of
the church to insure its place of power over

the serfs. The Lords accomplished this by having the churches preach that serfs were serfs because that is the way God meant it to be. Anyone who thought otherwise must be against God, and thus evil, would be dealt with swiftly and severely. This philosophy, in some instances, led to accusations of witchcraft. One of the most famous or infamous of these nonconformists was the French girl/soldier, Joan of Arc (Bois, 1999).

Joan of Arc was born in 1412 and lived only until her nineteenth birthday. "When she was twelve years of age, she began hearing voices of St. Michael, St. Catherine and St. Margaret believing them to be sent by God. These voices told her that it was her divine mission to free her country from the English, and help the dauphin gain the French throne", both of which Joan accomplished (Bois, 1999, p. 1).

However, in 1430 Joan was captured by the Burgundians an English ally and sold to the English. She was accused of being a witch and was subjected to fourteen months of imprisonment and questioning until convicted of heresy and witchcraft. She burned at the stake on May 30, 1431 (Bois, 1999).

How does the story of Joan of Arc add to the historical data concerning dissociation? Some of the descriptions of Joan's behavior was described as; hearing voices, responding to the voices, seeing apparitions that no one else could see, and speaking different voices including those of men and acting with male

mannerisms (Bois, 1999). These descriptions

mirror some of the behaviors of reported

dissociative behaviors but also other

conditions such as schizophrenia. Some

researchers wonder if Joan of Arc suffered

from multiple personality disorder, was

psychotic, or was truly a Saint who spoke

with God. The case study is interesting and

some of her behavior is similar to that of

sufferers of DID but the overall evidence

that Joan of Arc was dissociative is minimal.

In early America, the Salem witch trials

echoed the alliance of the State and

established religions. Citizens and leaders

often used accusations of witchcraft to rid

their community of undesirables and

nonconformists. Citizens, most often women were accused of unusual behaviors such as talking to the devil and having special powers that were used to harm others (Boese, 2004).

In Europe, these citizens were confronted by the authorities, and asked to prove their innocence. One example of a test was to throw the accused person in the lake. If the person sank, she was innocent, and if she floated, it proved that she was a witch (Boese, 2004)! Some researchers have put forth the idea that possibly these unfortunates were singled out for their unusual behaviors and may have been suffering from dissociative behavior. While this may be possible, the evidence points in my opinion, more often to petty jealousy or to protect themselves due to their own indiscretions. However, the practice of exorcism and reports of possession are not unheard of even in the twentieth and twenty-first centuries (Pratnicka, 2004).

Western Civilization's Psychological

Foundations

Related to Dissociation

This section of the literature review deals with text and documents found in the historical literature of Western civilization. The goal was to locate information that has affected the foundations of psychology in Europe and the United States as well as views concerning dissociative behavior.

The Western World experienced a growth of intellectual stimulation with the creation of universities in Western Europe in the twelfth century. This was a period of the Church and States working together and ruling by divine power. Some teachers, such as Galileo and others, found conflicting loyalties as they sought intellectual truth to understand man yet stay within the bounds of approved government and church doctrine.

Roger Bacon (1214-1292), one of many contributors to science and philosophy of this period, believed that "there are external and internal sense-oriented and spiritual experience is the only means of revealing the hidden forces through the three true operations sciences which are astrology, alchemy and magic" (Guniard, 2003 p.6). Magic was recognized as a science during this era. The boundaries between science and magic were nonexistent from the thirteenth century until the nineteenth century. One could even argue that there are still boundaries crossed between these two practices as scientists examine voodoo rituals in Haiti and their ability to create zombies.

Another scientist/philosopher of the time, Thomas Aquinas (1255-1274), believed that by using scientific proofs, one could demonstrate the existence of God. "Using proofs based on experience of sense-oriented reality and to enumerate the number of diverse attributes, the real is completely intelligible and truth consists of an alignment between things and words" (Guinard, 2003 p.7). Philosophers, teachers, doctors and others contributed to the ideas and writings to develop the foundation for the concepts of modern philosophy and psychology. These concepts include: the scientific method, field observation, the development and testing of theories, data collection, skepticism and other methods currently used by scientists.

Possible Evidence of Dissociation

The term dissociation was first used by Theophrateus Bombastus Von Hohenheim, a chemist, to describe the reactions of some compounds when subjected to heat. These compounds were described as dissociating or separating into pure compounds when heated to certain temperatures that affected their composition. Theophrateus was also known as Paracelsus and the complexities of human behavior interested him as well as chemistry. He is often credited as recording the first reported case resembling DID in 1646 (Putnam, 1989). He described the case of a female hostess who was accused of stealing money, but she denied it and accused the chefs. When it was pointed out to her that her hand was bleeding, she was perplexed as to how she injured her hand. She did not have any memory of what had taken place but when her injuries were pointed out to her, she no longer denied that she had stolen the box (Putnam, 1989). While this behavior could be attributed to other explanations, it was cited in several books as an early case study related to dissociation (Gurnard, 2003).

In 1791, Eberhardt Gmelin detailed his first case which he referred to as detachment. He documented the case of a twenty-one-year-old woman who was born in Germany and had neither been to France nor had ever learned to speak French. But suddenly, she spoke perfect French and believed herself to be a native Frenchwoman. Using hypnosis or magnetic sleep, Gmelin successfully treated the woman for her condition of an exchange of personalities (Greaves, 1993). Cases of this nature would soon be dealt with by a new kind of treatment that would change the field of psychology forever.

Any discussion of effective treatment
for Dissociative Identity Disorder must
include the topic of hypnosis. This tool has
been accepted as an invaluable tool in
releasing memories that have been banished to
the mind's gulag to protect the self.
Although the term hypnosis was first used in
1842 by Dr. Braid, the practice of hypnosis
and trances has been passed down and used in
African, Australian, and Egyptian cultures
for many generations (Bryan, 1963).

The earliest report of hypnotic trances
in Europe was found in the writings of an
Englishman, Dr. James Esdalie, who wrote,

Hypnosis in Medicine and Surgery. In this
book, he described a method of anesthesia
used by a famous Egyptian magician of his era
in Bengal. The magician had a reputation for
treating hysteria. He was introduced by the
Deputy Magistrate with the unforgettable name
of Baboo Essanchunder Ghosaul. Dr. Esdalie
suggested that the two magicians exchange
their knowledge about treating hysteria.
After some intervention by the Magistrate,
the Bengal magician agreed (Bryan, 1963).

        The Indian used what amounted to pre-
hypnosis relaxation by slowly stroking the
patient with leaves. As he did this, he
muttered incantations. After about an hour
of this preparation, he placed the person in
a trace and gave instructions for overcoming

hysteria. It was now the Englishman's turn, and he persuaded the magician to assist him. To relax the magician, he repeated the English song titled, "Kings of the Cannibal Island" (Bryan, 1963, p.1).

After a brief period, the Moolah became startled and wanted to stop the process. He was very upset and grabbed his head saying that he felt drunk. The next day, the two magicians compared their experiments, and the Englishman told the Moolah that he was too strong for his powers. The Moolah responded that just the opposite was the case, and he was, in fact, under the Englishman's powers (Bryan, 1963).

Later, when reviewing the Moolah's techniques, it was concluded that both, were

basically the same. After a period of
relaxing the hysterical patient through the
use of distraction, the patients were both
susceptible to suggestions through the use of
hypnosis. In what may be Western arrogance,
Dr. Esdalie claimed that the Moolah was not
totally aware of how his own techniques
really worked. "It convinced me that if
these charmers ever do well by such means, it
is by the Mesmeric influence probably unknown
to themselves" (Bryan, 1963, p.2)

     There is also documented use of
hypnosis-like treatment by Father Gassner of
the Catholic Church in the mid seventeen-
seventies. Father Gassner believed that the
illness was caused by possession (Bryan,
1963). With the church's approval, he sought

to cast out the devils by magnetizing patients using a metal crucifix. Father Gassner was reported to be very open to physicians observing his techniques. This openness permitted Franz Anton Mesmer to observe Father Gassner's hypnotic techniques.

In one case of an exorcism performed by Father Gassner, physicians were brought into a room that was like a theatre and seated. Then, the patient was brought onstage. Father Gassner, dressed in a long black cape and holding a golden crucifix, walked slowly onto the platform. The patient had been told that when Father Gassner touched him with the crucifix, he would fall onto the floor. While his patient lay on the floor, he would drive out the evil (Bryan, 1963).

Then, an observing physician examined the patient. He reported that the prostrate patient had felt no pulse or heart sounds, so he pronounced him dead. Father Gassner would then order the demon to depart and soon the patient would appear to be cured. Dr. Franz Anton Mesmer was reported to have witnessed several of these exorcisms in 1770 (Bryan, 1963).

Dr. Franz Mesmer did not believe that demons were the cause of illness or hysteria. Rather, he thought that the use of the magnetized crucifix played a part in the healing. Mesmer altered Father Gassmer's approach, but the essence was the same. Using a method of relation, focus, magnets, and repeated suggestion, Mesmer found that a patient could be cured of illnesses.

However, as with many innovations discovered

before and after Dr. Mesmer's, professional

jealousy and controversy forced him to flee

his practice in Vienna (Bryan, 1963).

While in Vienna, Mesmer had an

interesting case of his own, that was

believed to demonstrate the usefulness of

hypnosis in treating hysteria. "In 1777, Mara

Theresa Paradis, a blind child pianist and

favorite of the Empress, had her sight

restored after being treated by Mesmer. She

had been under the care of Europe's leading

eye specialist, Dr. Van Stoerckj, for more

than ten years without any improvement.

However, due to other doctors who became

jealous of Mesmer's influence with the

Empress, Mara's mother took her away from his care. In an emotional scene, the mother struck the child across the face because she did not wish to leave Dr. Mesmer's clinic and soon the hysterical blindness returned "(Bryan, 1963, p.4).

In 1784, the French Government formed a committee to investigate Mesmer's claims. Among those on the committee was an American, Ben Franklin; Monsieur Guillotin, the inventor of the Guillotine; and Dr. Lavoisier, a French chemist. The majority of the committee pronounced his theory of animal magnetism a fraud. Mesmer soon left France to travel to England, Italy, Germany and finally Switzerland, where he died (Bryan, 1963).

The increased acceptance and use of hypnosis in the professional community is widely credited to Dr. Jean Martin Charcot of the French Academy of Paris. He was born in France in 1825. Charcot was a well-known and respected professor at the University of Paris for 33 years and became Sigmund Freud's mentor in the use of hypnosis. As a world-renowned neurologist, he had a special interest in an illness termed hysteria (Van Der Hart, 2000).

The disorder was thought to be of mental origin with physical symptoms. He would place the patient under hypnosis in order to calm the patient and attempt to learn what events may have led to the hysteria. The historical background of the use, methods, and case studies by some pioneers in the field of psychology are cited due to the prominent role hypnosis plays in the treatment of DID.

Two other prominent, early theorists in the field of psychology who used hypnosis with patients were Pierre Janet and Sigmund Freud. Born in Paris in 1859, Janet studied philosophy at the Sorbonne. His true interest being medicine, he studied at the hospital of Le Havre, where he studied hypnosis. He became interested in the study of hysterical neurosis and read the research of Jean Charcot on the subject. At the age of thirty, Charcot appointed Pierre Janet Director of the Laboratory of Pathological Psychology at the Salpetriere Hospital. Janet continued to use hypnosis as a tool to treat hysteria. In 1889, he introduced the French term desagration or dissociation, to describe that which had previously been called hysterical conversion (Bryan, 1963).

Sigmund Freud initially was fascinated with hypnosis as a treatment tool, yet over time became less enthusiastic about the use of hypnosis. This may have been due to his cancer of the mouth, which made it difficult to say the lengthy pre-hypnotic relaxation phrases required as a part of the hypnotic treatment (Fisher, 2004).

One of the most commonly discussed medical cases of hysteria where hypnosis was used is that of Anna O. Anna, a patient of Dr. Josef Breuer, was suffering from hysteria and, at times, paralysis. Dr. Breuer consulted with Dr. Freud. Although born and raised in Germany, at times, she would speak only English or French. When thirsty, she could or would not drink. These were just some of the behaviors that mirrored DID and that Breuer and Freud encountered in Anna O (Van Der Hart, 2000).

Was Anna O a patient suffering from DID? We do not know but many of her behaviors mirror some of the behaviors of these dissociative patients today. The use of hypnosis is still commonly used in the treatment of DID in order to retrieve the memories of those suffering from Post-Traumatic Stress Syndrome (PTSS) that often precedes Dissociation.

It is important to note that there was a backlash, in the late eighteen-hundreds, in part fueled by Freud's reluctance to use hypnosis. Also, some patients were found to be faking the condition of hysteria (Bryan 2003). Rather than progress in the search for a better understanding of hysteria, a new debate raged.

That debate continues today. Dr. Paul R. McHugh, Professor of Psychiatry and Director of the Department of Psychiatry and Behavioral Science at the John Hopkins Medical Institution in Baltimore, is a skeptic of DID. In response to the question, "Does DID exist?", he cited this incident that took place at the Salpetriere Hospital in Paris in the 1880's.

Jean-Martin Charcot, the chief physician, had thought that he had discovered a new disease called "hystero-epilepsy", a mind and brain disorder. Joseph Babinski, a skeptical student, decided that Charcot had invented rather than discovered hystero-epilepsy. These patients of Charcot were housed together and convinced by Charcot that they suffered from this new disease. Babinski believed that these patients, being highly suggestible, mirrored the behavior of these attacks. He convinced Charcot to separate the patients and once done, the attacks ceased. Next, he injected a counter-suggestion to give the patient a different diagnosis. This also altered the behaviors of the patient's based on the counter-suggestion. Babinski argued that doctors could invent diseases then persuade patients to mirror the same symptoms of the disease to give credibility to the disease (McHugh, 2001 p.1).

As put forth by Babinski in 1880, Dr. McHugh also believes that DID is created by today's therapists. This is based on his observation of tapes of therapeutic sessions that he claims demonstrates the creation of DID by the therapists' manipulation.

The early pioneers in the field did not differentiate between dissociative phenomenon and hysterical conversion. Morton Prince, the renowned neuropsychiatrist, has been called the Father of Multiple Personality Syndrome. His studies led him to also note the similarities between the hysteria of the 1800s and Multiple Personality Disorder. Rather than MPD, the condition was termed secondary personality in the early 1900s (Prince, 1906).

1. The debate over the existence of secondary personalities continued into the twentieth century. In 1907, Janet found that most reported cases of multiple personalities were from America. Janet concluded that multiple personality was a psychological condition which was endemic to the United States. He attributed this outbreak to the influence of Psychologists and other mental health professionals, the high exposure of the American public to stories about MPD, the acceptance of Americans to engage in

role play and the tendency of Americans to be more introspective than other cultures (Morris, 1989). This debate was postponed by world events, which greatly changed the lives of these theorists. One such event was the World War I experience of many soldiers that lead to a dramatic change in the views on Multiple Personality Disorder.

The Impact of War Trauma

One result of war is the opportunity to gather great quantities of documentation of the impact that severe stress and trauma have on human beings. World War I, optimistically labeled the war to end all wars, was just the beginning of generations of hostilities that have resulted in millions of physical and

mental injuries. The injured included
civilians and soldiers alike. The following
description of life as a soldier in World War
I creates a vivid picture of a soldier's
daily trials.

Fighting a modern war means to entrench
yourself in a hole filled with water and to
sit in it for ten days without moving, it
means looking and listening and keeping a
grenade in your hand, it means eating cold
food and sinking in the mud and carrying your
food through the dark night and wandering
hour after hour around the same point without
ever finding it, it means being hit by
grenades which come from God know where - in
short, it means privation (Van Der Hart, 2000
pg. 10).

This description leaves out the horror of rats eating men as they sleep, the decayed corpses of friends that lay in the trenches, the wounded men screaming for help from outside the barbed wire, and the inability to change any of these things. There was no personal or public sanitation. Those men not wounded were suffering from dysentery, malaria, lack of food, lack of sleep, trench foot and other diseases (Van Der Hart, 2000).

While the physical deprivations suffered during war is horrific, the emotional stress may be even greater. Many veterans of war say that the smell of war is their strongest memory. The odor of decaying bodies, mixed with urine and feces, is overwhelming and unforgettable. The air also carries the

scent of gunpowder and burning flesh and
lingers for hours. World War I veterans also
remember the first scent of poison gas as
they rushed to locate and put on their gas
masks.

These living conditions were combined
with the necessity to leave the safety of the
despicable trenches to enter a killing zone.
If the soldier, by some miracle, made it
safely to the enemy trenches, he most often
faced a next test of his strength, skill, and
resolve to kill the enemy with his rifle,
knife, bare hands, or any other means
possible. His reward was survival until he
was ordered to repeat this horrific task.

It is reported that the defeated Central
powers lost 3,500,000 soldiers while the

victorious allied powers lost 5,100,000 men in World War I. The casualty rate in the first day of the Battle of the Somme was 20,000 men killed for the British Army (Gilbert, 1995 p.541).

The field doctors used a variety of terms to label the mental casualties of war. Shell shock, neurasthenia, war neurosis or, in German, Kriegsneuroser, were coined in an effort to give general terms to the mental illnesses (Van Der Hart, 2000, p.6).

The ignorance about the actual impact that the conditions of war have on a human being was proven early on in World War I. Many soldiers suffering shock, fatigue and other results from battle were labeled cowards and malingerers, court marshaled and then sent to prison or even shot! The armies on both sides soon took a step back to review what was occurring as thousands of brave, battle- proven men began to suffer emotional breakdowns from the accumulative effects of months of action on the battlefields.

"It was believed, even by Freud in 1919, that with the end of the war, most of the neurotic diseases that had been brought about by the war disappeared" (Van Der Hart, 2000 p.42). However, some veterans and psychiatrist, Robert Gaup, felt differently. Of all the of German soldiers wounded during the war, 617,000 men, suffered from war trauma. Entire companies suffered from vomiting, and fits of crying (Van Bergen, 1999). The British statistics were much smaller; 80,000 men diagnosed as suffering from war neuroses. The British credit the great variances to an under-reporting (Van Bergen, 1999). Though few longitudinal studies followed the outcome of these cases, it was clear to all that the development of mental disorders may, be related to traumatic experiences (Witztum, 2004).

In 1929, aides who worked assisting World War I veterans in the mental ward of an English hospital wrote: "During the recent war, a great mass of illness occurred which, christened at first by the misleading name of shell shock, came ultimately to be known as psychoneuroses of war" (Shepard, 2001, pg 494). This change of nomenclature was due to the rapidly won recognition of the psychological origin of these conditions. Indeed, it may be said that, "whatever else the war has done, it has at least conclusively demonstrated the existence and importance of psychogenic disorder" (Shepard, 2001 p.494).

In 1919, Dr. Brown, a physician in a Bristol Veterans Hospital in England, wrote, "viewed from the psychological point of view, hysterical disorders all fall under one heading, as examples of dissociation of psycho-physical functions: (walking, speaking, hearing, remembering) (Brown, W.,1919 p.833). Likewise, Dr. Meyers, in nineteen-forty, formulated the concept that the "functional nervous disorders are assignable to a dissociated personality and it results" (Meyers, 1940 p.316). Thus, the understanding of DID as a coping reaction to trauma became more credible in the realm of psychology.

The physicians sought Pierre Janet's assistance in attempting to understand what was occurring, as a result of these war traumas. A form of mental depression, characterized by retraction of the field of consciousness (involuntary and intense narrowing of attention), and a tendency to the dissociation and emancipation of the systems of ideas and functions that constitute the personality, was one of Janet's observations. (Janet, 1920)

Another valuable insight into dissociation was based on observations of war injuries. The reduction in the victim's level of consciousness, as a result of facing these traumas reduces the person's ability to integrate experiences. This is one factor, that occurs prior to the onset of dissociation. Meyers (1940) pointed out that the normal personality is in abeyance. Even if it is acceptable to receiving impressions, it shows no signs of responding to them. The recent traumatic experiences of the individual and his usual behavior have been replaced by, what may be referred to as, the emotional personality. Gradually, or suddenly, an apparently normal personality usually returns except for the lack of all memory of events directly connected with the trauma that resulted in the dissociation.

Sometimes there are alternations to the emotional and the apparently normal personalities. Upon its return, the apparently normal personality may recall distressing experiences revived during the temporary intrusion of the emotional personality. The emotional personality may also return during sleep; the functional disorders of mutism, paralysis, and contracture that are usually not apparent. Upon waking, however, the apparently normal personality may have no recollection of a dream state and will, at once resume his previous condition of disability (Meyers, 1940 pp.66-67).

World War II, Korea, Vietnam and Gulf

Wars

The impact on modern psychology, research and recognition of dissociative behavior resulting from severe trauma was well documented in World War I. The soldiers of World War II, at least in the United States, faced a battery of tests that were designed to sort out the mentally misfit who were joining the service. Presently, due to the increased number of World War II and Korean veterans dying due to age, more and more of war veteran studies in the United States and Britain are turning to Viet Nam and Gulf War veterans (Langer, 1998).

"From the American Civil War through the Viet Nam War, combat veterans have suffered from soldiers' heart, irritable heart, effort syndrome, battle fatigue, combat neuroses, and shell shock" (Langer, 1998 p.1). While these conditions were often overlooked, or not seen as important to treat as physical wounds, the post-World War I experience with these conditions changed the way the next generation of soldiers was treated. Each war has its own unique emotional and physical challenges and rules of engagement. In the United States Civil War, the fighting often involved family members fighting friends, cousins, or even brothers. Combat medicine was in its infancy and amputation was often the choice of treatment for arm and leg wounds. Hand-to-hand combat was frequent. World War I soldiers often never saw the enemy but saw the results of artillery, gas attacks, machine gun and the new tanks that reduced the personal side of war. However, trench warfare was a psychological enemy for all to fear. "World War II emphasized the physiological and psychological symptoms that formed the concept physioneurosis shortly after World War II when the DSM I produced the formal classification of reactions to severe combat" (p2). DSMII, III, and IIIR altered these classifications but each recognized the condition. DSM III diagnosed these symptoms as PTSD (Langer, 1998).

During the early 1920's, Abram Kardiner, an attending specialist at the Bronx Veterans Home, assisted World War I veterans. Prior to this appointment, he had studied hysteria under Freud in Vienna. He theorized that these veterans had developed a fixation on the trauma and could not resolve or integrate the incidents into their memory. He believed that a fixation from the trauma was created and the victim, "would act as if the original trauma was still in existence and would engage in protective mechanisms, including dissociation" (p4).

In the 1970's, more and more returning veterans of the Viet Nam War also exhibited PSTD symptoms and some reported cases of dissociation. The Viet Nam War was quite different from World War II or the Korean War. With no clear-cut territories to win and hold, the Viet Nam veterans were more involved with the general population in this guerilla war. It was not uncommon to see children killing soldiers and soldiers responding by killing children. Burning villages and torture were a part of this war. The methods of war in Viet Nam were very contrary to the soldiers' American values. These behavior patterns fit the psychological profile of traumatic experiences that can lead to dissociation (Langer, 1998).

In several studies, (Tomb in 1994, Roszell, McFall and Malos in 1991, and Bremner, Southwick, Brett, Fontana, Rosencheck, and Charney in 1992), researched the connections between combat PTSD and dissociation. Each using scientific data collection found that,

"the scores of the PTSD patients, veterans,
were almost double those of the non-PTSD
patients in regards to dissociative symptoms"
(Langer, 1998 p 2).

The identical result was found by,
McCarroll, Ursano and Fullerton in a 1995
study regarding certain Gulf War situations
and dissociation and PTSD. Veterans who had
to deal with recovery of the war dead were
assessed. Once again, those in the study who
had the task of recovering war dead had
higher levels of PTSD and Dissociative
symptoms than soldiers not involved with this
gruesome task (Langer, 1998).

Dissociation was not limited or caused
only by childhood trauma, as these
researchers discovered. Trauma, in general,

which the mind refuses to integrate in the memory seems to be a strong cause for dissociative protective coping. In the conclusions of a study, by Rosen, Fields, Hands, in 1989, investigating the relationship between war trauma and PTSD, even after forty years, up to 50 per cent of veterans showed signs of PTSD. "The perspectives of these veterans differed by not the impact of the trauma. World War II vets suffered more anxiety, feelings of estrangement, withdrawal and sleep disturbance. The Viet Nam vets experienced nightmares, or dissociative phenomena such as flashbacks" (Langer, 1998 p4).

The debate of whether war trauma can cause dissociative coping behavior seemed put to rest. In another study of the connection

of combat trauma to PTSD and DID, Mellman,

Brawman, Olga, Flores and Melanes (1992)

turned their attention to suggested factors

of predisposition of individuals to PTSD and

Dissociative behavior. It was suggested that

a dysfunction in the neurotransmitters could

underline PTSD (Langer 1998).

In 1994, several events took place to

add to the history of MPD/DID. The criteria

in DSM III-R, used for a diagnosis of MPD,

was changed and the new term for the

diagnosis was also changed to Dissociative

Identity Disorder. In that same year, ASD or

Acute Stress Disorder was added to DSM IV.

ASD's symptoms are similar to PTSD, however,

the diagnosis of this ailment is limited to

the first thirty days after a traumatic event (Gibson, 2004). The connection of ASD and dissociation is that dissociative symptoms are the key difference between a diagnosis of PTSD and ASD. Three specific indicators of dissociative behavior, numbing, reduced awareness, derealization and/or amnesia, must be present for a diagnosis of ASD. The addition of this diagnosis to DSM IV changes the recognition of the existence of dissociation from a condition whose existence is in doubt, to a condition that is recognized as required for another condition to exist (Gibson, 2004). The most recent version of DSM is DSM-IV-TR, published in 2000 this is a minor revision of DSM IV. DSM-V, is scheduled to be published in 2010

(Gibson, 2004).

The history and understanding of the conditions previously known as Multiple Personality Disorder and currently Dissociative Identity Disorder are still in their infancy. The establishment of the criteria for MPD in the Diagnostic Statistical Manual occurred only twenty-four years ago. The use of dissociative behavior in the diagnosis for Acute Stress Disorder is only ten years old (Ross, 1989).

What future changes in the diagnoses and treatment of DID can be predicted? As the history of this condition continues into the twenty-first century, Dissociation and MPD, are viewed by some as separate and distinct conditions, yet as interchangeable diagnoses by others (Ross, 1989). Current literature supports the supposition that dissociation, could be evaluated on a continuum as put forth by Dr. Braun. This continuum consists of daydreaming and highway hypnosis at one extreme, and completely separate personalities, that alternate control over the host as the other extreme (Braun, B., 1988).

One trend that appears to be gaining momentum in the research is a move towards focusing on developing and providing early diagnosis, better therapy, and improved training for therapists. The condition of DID will no longer be seen as a rare coping behavior but as an understandable reaction to survive severe trauma (McHugh, 2001).

However, caution should be taken, not to

dismiss the dwindling protestations of the

naysayers who claim that dissociation is an

iatrogenic condition.

Case Studies in America of Multiple

Personality Disorder and Dissociative

Identity Disorder

The first documented report, in America,

of possible multiple personalities was the

case of Mary Reynolds, who displayed two

personalities. The case was publicized in

1830 by Robert Macnish. Mary Reynolds was

born in 1785 in Pennsylvania. The first

symptoms of her illness occurred one morning

in 1811. Rather than the stoic young lady

her family and friends had known for years,

they encountered an energetic and social lady quite different in speech and mannerisms than they had ever seen. This went on for five weeks until she awoke and displayed her previous behavior. She had no memory of her behavior during the previous five weeks. Diagnosed as a multiple personality, Mary continued to alternate between these behaviors until, at age thirty-six, the docile personality remained constant for the rest of her life. What made this case unique, in addition to this first diagnosis of multiple personality in America, was that it was published in Harper's Weekly Magazine in 1906. Readers across the country became curious and interested and sought more information about this unusual story of behavior (Wozniak, 1906).

A second case, documented in the nineteenth century in the United States, was that of Ansel Bourne in 1887. In 1857, the young Ansel Bourne was asked if he would attend a prayer meeting. He responded, "I would rather be struck deaf and dumb forever" (Salter, 1961 Ch8.p1). Reportedly, his wish was granted, and he was deaf and mute for the next thirty days. He later responded to a voice that told him to serve God, and he became a preacher for the next twenty-five years. In early 1887, he withdrew several hundred dollars to purchase chase land in an area of Providence, Rhode Island. He was not heard from again until three months later in Norristown, Pennsylvania under the name

Albert J. Brown. Diagnosed as having multiple
personalities, Ansel Bourne was treated,by
William James, an associate of Morton Prince
(Salter, 1961).

Morton Prince (1854-1929), a graduate of
Harvard who later founded The Journal of
Abnormal Psychology, was a medical doctor
whose book, The Dissociation of a Personality
and the Subconscious, influenced America and
theories on personality. In his book, he
documented the case of Christine Beauchamps.
Ms. Beauchamps sought Prince's assistance for
fatigue and headaches. Prince, a neurologist,
stated that he interacted with several
personalities which he identified as BI, BII,
through BVIII. Dr. Prince used hypnosis as
part of the treatment and as a result,

several other personalities soon emerged. The diagnosis was, that as a result of trauma, Sally Beauchamp had created four separate personalities (Wozniak, 1906).

William James was also interested in these two cases and presented both case histories in his article, The Consciousness of Self, and in his book, The Principles. Some of the ideas and terms from this book are still relevant in helping us understand dissociation today. These terms can be found in explanations used today to explain how and why dissociation occurs. The theories and ideas of William James and Morton Prince are important pieces to a better understanding of the evolution of views regarding dissociation in nineteenth and twentieth century America (Wozniak, 1906).

Just as the publishing of the case of Mary Reynolds in Harper Magazine in 1906, the movie, Sybil, and the movie, The Three Faces of Eve, were to educate much of the American public regarding multiple personalities. In 1954, published in Dr. Morton Prince's, Journal of Abnormal Psychology, was the case of Chris Costner Sizemore. In 1957, Corbett Thigpen and Harvey Clechly wrote the book, The Three Faces of Eve, based on the life story of Chris Sizemore (Greaves, 1993). Ms. Sizemore wrote several books describing her case and appeared on ABC Television on March 4, 1998. Three events were claimed to have led to the dissociation of Ms. Sizemore. She witnessed a gruesome death in a sawmill;

several years later found a corpse in a

ditch; and the final event was the death of a

beloved family member (Greaves, 1993).

Another case study that led to a book

and later, a movie, is the case of Sybil

Isabel Dorsett. In this case, Sybil is said

to have suffered physical, sexual, and

emotional abuse as a child at the hands of

her mother.

The movie, Sybil, arrived in theatres

during a time when clinicians and researchers

were devoting research to the topic of MPD.

Dr. Ellenberger published, The Discovery of

the Unconscious: The History and Evolution

of Dynamic Psychiatry. This publication was

followed by the book, Therapy of Multiple

Personality, written by Margareta Bowers.

Many of the ideas and rules for treating

Dissociation today are based on this text.

Yet, it was the case of Sybil Isabel

Dorsett that is considered "the most

important clinical case of MPD in the

twentieth century" (Greaves, 1993 p.363). The

book written by Flora Rheta and soon was

followed by the movie, of the same name,

starring Sally Field as Sybil. The movie's

scenes of child abuse were the most explicit

ever seen by a national audience. Horrific

scene after scene showed a young girl at the

mercy of a sick and deranged mother who beat

and sexually tortured her daughter

unmercifully. After witnessing this abuse, it

was clear to most observers how and why a

person would split into other personalities

(Greaves, 1993).

The description of the incidents that lead to Dr. Wilbur's diagnosis of Sybil's MPD were as follows:

"One day, when she was talking to me about something that should have made her angry, she jumped off the couch, went over and stuck her fist through one of the windowpanes in my office. I jumped out of my chair, ran over, grabbed her wrist and said, 'Let me see if you cut yourself.' She ducked down and hunched her shoulders, peered up at me and said, 'Let me go.' I said, 'No, I want to see your hand, and if you cut yourself.' She looked at me and said, 'Am I more important than the window?' I said, 'Certainly. A handyman can fix the window, but if you are cut, it would take a doctor to sew you up.' She had not cut herself, but she was not talking like her typical self. She looked younger and frightened, so I asked her a spontaneous question, 'Who are you?' She said, 'I am Peggy.' I thought immediately that this must be a dual personality, but I said nothing to the patient about this." "The next time this patient was due in the office, I opened the door, and here was a young woman in high heels, hair piled on top of her head, very elegant looking, who looked at me and said, 'I am sorry, Sybil was ill today, so I came -- I am Vicky.' I said, 'Come in,' and during this hour 'Vicky' apprised me of the fact that, yes there is 'Peggy' and herself and 'others' as well as Sybil, but I should not tell Sybil this because it would upset her. So here I was with a Multiple Personality, never having diagnosed one before, never having treated one, and not really knowing what to do. I was, as usual, very excited about this new kind of case" (as cited in Burnett, 2003, p.2).

Wilbur continued working with Sybil and wrote papers on dissociation and hysteria and multiple personality, but she could not get her papers published (Burnett, 2003). After more than sixteen years of work with Sybil,

Dr. Wilbur learned that Sybil was the victim of horrific abuse inflicted on her by her psychotic mother. Her father failed to protect her from her mother's abuse. As a result, she developed alter personalities which embodied feelings and emotions the real Sybil could not cope with. The waking Sybil was deprived of all these emotions, and was, therefore, a rather drab figure. She was unaware of her other personas; while they were in control of the body, Sybil suffered blackouts and did not remember the episodes. Cornelia Wilbur helped Sybil integrate the personalities. Denied the ability to publish her work in professional journals of the time, Wilbur invited Schreiber to write the popularized account of Sybil's case (Greaves,

1993).

The case of Sybil is significant in several respects. Sybil's psychiatrist, Cornelia Wilbur, went to great lengths to validate the accounts of abuse including interviews with Sybil's parents, a visit with Sybil to her childhood home, and speaking with Sybil's doctor and reviewing his records (Greaves, 1993). The case firmly linked multiple personality disorder with child abuse (Gold, 1993). Wilbur's therapy, which included hypnosis and other therapeutic interventions produced a successful resolution, was used, as an example for many multiples and their therapists (Putnam, 1989).

Another high-profile case in America not

only kept MPD in the public eye, but it resulted in a historic court decision. In the mid-nineteen seventies, the name Billy Milligan made headlines across the United States. Billy was born in 1955 in Ohio. His traumas began three years later when his father committed suicide in 1958. His mother, suffering from depression and anxiety, often locked Billy in the cupboard. He was sexually and physically abused by his stepfather. As a child, Billy displayed various symptoms that today are accepted as symptoms of Dissociation, yet these symptoms may have been misdiagnosed. In 1970, he was placed in an Ohio state hospital for mental illness, but was later released (Keyes, 1981).

One evening, in 1977, on the campus of Ohio State University, Adelana, Billy's lesbian personality in need of love and affection, committed the rapes of three Ohio State students. Upon his examination by a county psychiatrist, Billy was diagnosed as suffering from Multiple Personality Disorder and eventually diagnosed as having at least twenty-four personalities. Each of these personalities had their own voice, personal history, character, and was an individual distinct person (Keyes, 1981).

While preparing for the trial, the defense team claimed Billy was insane at the time due to Multiple Personality Disorder. Billy Milligan was found innocent by reason of insanity using MPD as a defense. He was released from Moritz Prison for the Criminally Insane in 1988, after being incarcerated for ten years. The state reported that all of his personalities had integrated into one. Billy Milligan now lives in Los Angeles and manages a production company. This was the first successful use of MPD by a defense team in a criminal trial in the United States (Noll, 2002).

One case, involving the United States Government, is detailed, in the book Project Bluebird, written by Colin Ross. This story is based on documents released from the Central Intelligence Agency (CIA) under the Freedom of Information Act (FOIA). The book describes how the CIA and other United States security agencies in the early 1950's were concerned about the success of the Russians, Chinese, and North Koreans to brainwash captured United States personnel (Ross, 2000).

The blueprint for creating multiples, was based on captured documents from Nazi psychologists and doctors. The FOIA documents describe the reason and method for creating multiple personalities in United States citizens. To combat brainwashing and torture that the Russians had learned from captured Nazis, the United States Central Intelligence Agency sought to develop agents with MPD to counter the Russians methods of prisoner interrogation (Ross, 2000).

By creating several personalities within an individual, the United States Government sought to protect and deliver top secret information. In one case, an agent was created as a multiple through a series of physically and sexually abusive situations. He was later hypnotized and asked to speak as one identity, which was given the code and told not to reveal it to anyone but his contact in Russia. Then another personality was sent to Russia, totally unaware that another personality had the information. If the agent was captured and tortured, the risk of divulging any secrets was greatly reduced (Ross, 2000). This information is very important to the understanding of DID since it claims to prove to understand not only how DID occurs but that it can be created!

     Each of these cases was a well-documented case of dissociation diagnosed in the United States during the twentieth century. Based on the documentation of these and other numerous cases, the debate over whether the mind resorts to Dissociative behavior in the face of severe trauma is not at as great an issue of debate as it was in the past. Whether referred to as hysteria, Multiple Personality Disorder, or Dissociative Identity Disorder, there is agreement among a great number of therapists and professors that this condition does exist. It is now important to focus the debate on how to successfully diagnose and treat these victims of various devastating traumas whose minds have resorted to dissociation as a means of survival.

CHAPTER 3: SUMMARY AND RECOMMENDATIONS

Summary of Literature Review

Over a two-year period, more than eight hundred books and hundreds of journal articles, internet websites and various other sources were reviewed in the search for information relevant to the history of multiple personality disorder/dissociation. The literature review resulted in the locating and consolidating of information from ancient, medieval, pre- and post- World War eras to the present. The ideas of theorists long recognized as contributing to various psychological theories spanning more than one hundred years included James, Breuer, S. Freud, A. Freud, Prince, Ross,

Charcot, Janet, Turhis, Greaves, Kluftand and others were reviewed for their thoughts and theories on hysteria and dissociation. The result of this process: a document that presents the history of Dissociative Identity Disorder that will assist therapists and patients alike to better understand DID. In addition to this goal, there were several research questions to be answered in the literature review.

The first question was, "Is there a history of documented cases that contain evidence of Dissociative Identity Disorder?" The answer is that numerous documented cases were found in various eras that could be interpreted as possible evidence of dissociative behavior. However, the pre-

Freudian eras did not provide noteworthy
literature that provided significant
contributions to the base of knowledge to
understand dissociation. In this literature,
there were few descriptions of human behavior
that could be interpreted as evidence of
Dissociative Identity Disorder. The
descriptions could be attributed to
schizophrenia or numerous other personality
illnesses.

In the Freudian and post-Freudian eras,
there was a distinct difference in the number
of and quality of reports when compared to
the pre-Freudian eras. This is due to a
dedication to detailed documentation and the
use of scientific methods. Also, there were
numerous books, case studies, and other

literature available from various researchers that provide documentation of dissociative behavior after a person faced extreme trauma.

During and after World War I, there was significant documentation of hundreds of thousands of cases related to war trauma, Post Traumatic Stress Disorder and dissociative behavior. These case studies resulted in documentation of behavior that created the necessary documentation that verified a connection between severe trauma and dissociation as a coping behavior in reaction to the trauma. This pattern of dissociative behavior related to PTSD continues in trauma victims from war, hostage situations, the 9/11 terrorist attacks, rape and other similar situations. This data provides a great deal of evidence of the existence of Dissociative Identity Disorder.

The second research question was, "When was the theory of MPD first put forth?" In the literature search to answer this question, the search led back to World War I. "DSM I (Diagnostic and Statistical Manual of Mental Disorders Version I) was created after World War I to provide a framework for labeling post-war psychiatric causalities. DSM II was written after World War II for the same purposes" (Allison 1996). These manuals were composed by members of the American Psychiatric Association and then reviewed and printed by the distributors of the International Code of Diseases (ICD).

In DSM II, MPD was listed under

hysterical dissociative disorder and did not have its own code. In 1980, DSM III was written and later revised in 1997 as DSM III-R. In DSM III, MPD was officially given its own code number and was described by specific characteristics. As one therapist said, "If it is listed in here, it must exist" (Allison, 1996, p.2).

Prior to the writing of DSM IV, there was a conference in 1994 of the American Psychiatric Association (APA). One of the topics discussed was how MPD should be described in the new manual. The committee was made up of two groups who disagreed over the definition of MPD. Those who were professors and instructors wanted to eliminate MPD because, as one professor said,

"Everyone is born with only one personality. Therefore, there can be no such thing as MPD" (Allison, 1996, p.3).

However, the psychiatrists, who were therapists, could not accept this argument. These therapists consistently observed patients who, they claimed, did have totally different personalities. Not only different personalities, but some patient's characters had different diseases, blood pressure readings, names and even family histories. Based on these observations, these therapists believed that their clients did have separate and multiple personalities.

The professors claimed that rather than treat patients by integrating personalities, the therapists should address the delusion that there was more than one identity. The

professors and instructors won the debate,

and the condition was identified as

Dissociative Identity Disorder. However, the

debate wasn't over yet. When the new ICD-9

was printed, it listed both terms, to be used

interchangeably (Allison 1996).

The third research question was, "How

was the behavior that today is diagnosed as

DID been documented in the past?" The answer

to this question was found in the review of

the literature to answer the first question.

Prior to the 1800s, much of the

documentation, was based on stories, tales

and poorly written and or transcribed

records. Some records appear tainted based

on other factors that influenced the authors

such as religious concerns. It was not until
the development and use of the scientific
method by theorists such as Charcot, Janet,
Freud, Breuer and others that detailed
observations and record keeping improved in
the field of psychology.

The fourth question asked was,
"Specifically, what is the history of
Multiple Personality Disorder/ Dissociative
Identity Disorder in the United States?" It
was interesting to see the role that the
media played in the history of MPD/DID in the
United States. While many professors,
therapists and others interested in
psychology read various books on the subject,
it was the mass media that is credited with
informing the general public about multiple

personality disorder. First, there was the nationally distributed story on 1906 in Harpers Bazaar Weekly about Mary Reynolds. This was followed by two world wars that resulted in many veterans returning home to families who sought answers to understand these soldiers' new behaviors and changes in personalities. Two other media events were to educate the American public during the nineteen fifties and nineteen sixties as Harpers Bazaar had done in nineteen hundred and six. The case studies of Eve and Sybil were shared with the American public in two books, a television story and a motion picture. This resulted in the further education of the American public to multiple personality disorder.

Based, in part, on these events, some therapists and patients alike saw an increase in other diagnoses of MPD. The awareness of this diagnosis drew greater attention as public defenders sought to use MPD as a defense strategy for murder cases. In 1971, Billy Milligan was found innocent of rape and murder due to insanity and a diagnosis of MPD. MPD was again in the national limelight, news, and law books.

The courts and movies were to again play a role in forming the public belief and views on MPD and dissociation. Several accused murderers attempted to feign MPD in order to use the Milligan strategy to escape conviction. These scenarios were brought to life in the movies _Identity_ and _Primal Fear_, which showed how it was possible to fake MPD. As the American public used various books, movies and newscasts to learn about MPD over the years, changes to the DSM showed the therapists and professors changes in the theories and philosophies about MPD. In 1994, in DSM IV, MPD, was officially recognized as a separate psychological condition (Allison 1996).

More recently, in the late nineteen-hundreds and early twenty-first century, the breaking of the DNA code has influenced the theories about how personality is formed. More emphasis is being credited to genetic influence over environmental impact. There are also books documenting government studies, such as Bluebird by Colin Ross, that have evidence that MPD and dissociation can be intentionally created under controlled conditions. This result is credited to the United States Central Intelligence Agency in its search to protect secrets.

Finally, there is the use of all the historical information, theories, and data to develop new treatments and medications to assist sufferers of DID and MPD. While the most recent DSM edition lists these two terms interchangeably, some theorists are citing clear differences between these two conditions. It is safe to say that many more changes, and new theories regarding DID and MPD are forthcoming.

Recommendations for Future Research

The first recommendation is to establish a national clearing house for reporting, storing, and reviewing case studies and information related to Dissociation. Currently, the International Society for the Study of Dissociative Identity Disorder, located in Chicago, is probably the most recognized authority in the United States on the topic of DID. However, no institution has attempted to collect and review data to verify its accuracy prior to publication or placement on the Internet. This would be invaluable in creating a large and accurate amount of data regarding the diagnosis and treatment of DID. This resource would be invaluable to layman and professionals alike.

The second recommendation is to collate and review a universally recognized and accepted dictionary of terminology related to DID. This would universalize the terminology and result in reducing the misunderstandings in research and diagnosis.

The final recommendation is the review of the International Society for the Study of Dissociation's treatment guidelines for DID by the American Psychiatric Association and American Medical Association as well as other organizations to standardize and improve the diagnosis and treatment of sufferers of DID. This literature review discovered numerous documents that give credibility to the diagnosis of Dissociative Identity Disorder. Now the challenge before the mental health community is to turn their resources and intellectual abilities to the treatment of this mental illness.

Implications for Social Change

The goal of this thesis literature review was to consolidate information from numerous sources on the history of Dissociation into one document. This document would provide researchers and laypeople with one resource that describes the history of Dissociation. The need for this resource, is based on several factors. First, there is a misunderstanding among many professionals and laypeople about what DID is, why it occurs, and the dynamics of this coping behavior. Secondly, the research on the topic is still relatively new and there are few resources that delve into significant depth on the history of DID. Thirdly, numerous instances of DID, related to war trauma, have been documented based on case studies from World War I to the current Gulf War conflict. The need for a better understanding and treatment of this coping phenomenon is critical to assisting current United States troops and their families as these veterans return home from the war.

The benefit of a better understanding of DID and MPD is not limited to veterans but also trauma victims in general. The terror attacks of September eleven have yielded additional victims who did not perish in the attack. These victims must also be helped to learn that you do not forget the trauma but, with help, learn to cope with the feelings that result from the trauma.

Violence in our society has increased, leading to other severe traumas such as rape, hostage-taking, murder and other instances that result in post-traumatic stress, a precursor of DID. DID is a coping option that therapists need to be prepared to diagnose and treat. This thesis adds to the information available to help reach these goals.

References

Allison, R. (1996) Dual Personality, What's in a Name? Homepage Ralph Allison Retrieved October 18, 2004 from http://www.dissociation.com/index/Definition

American Psychiatric Association. (2000) Diagnostic and Statistical Manual of Mental Disorders. Fourth Edition. Text Revision. Washington DC: American Psychiatric Association.

Boese, A. (2004). The witch trial at mount holly museum hoaxes.com. Retrieved September 3, 2004 from http://www.museumofhoaxes.com/witchtrial.html

Bois, D. (2003, April 2). Joan of arc. Distinguished women.com. Retrieved October 25, 2003, from www.distinguishedwomen.com/inds/hmtl

Braun, Bennett. (1988). The BASK model of dissociation. Dissociation Volume 1 number 1. March, 1988. Retrieved November 3, 2004 from http://www.inpsyte.ca/braun.html

Brown, W. (1919) War Neuroses: A comparison

of early cases seen in the field with those seen at the base. Columbus, Ohio: *The Lancet,* May 17,833-836.

Bryan, W. (1963). History of hypnosis. Retrieved March 26, 2004, from www.infinityinstitution.com.

Budge, E. W. (1895). The book of the dead, the papyrus of ani. Sacredtexts.com Retrieved February 15, 2004, from http://www.sacred-texts.com/egy/ebod/html

Burnett, N. (2003). *A history of the study of MPD/DID.* Retrieved January 26, 2004 from www.m-a-h.net/library/didgeneral/article-history.htm

CIA (2004) The world fact book. Retrieved October 12, 2004 from http://www.cia.gov/cia/publications/factbook/

Fisher, J. (2004) Freud and hypnosis. HypnoGenesis Retrieved on August 28, 2004 from http://www.hypnos.co.uk.hypnomag/

Gibson, L. (2004) Acute stress disorder. National center for PTSD. Retrieved October

15, 2004 from
http://www.ncptsd.org/facts/specific/fs-asd.html

Gilbert, M. (1995). The first world war. New York: Henry Holt Publishing.

Gold, J. (1993). (Cornelia B. Wilbur M.D.: An Appreciation) In clinical perspectives on multiple personality disorder. Washington, DC: American Psychiatric Press.

Greaves, G. (1993). A history of MPD. Washington, DC: American Psychological Press.

Guinard, P. (2003). *The ten stars of earliest Greek thought-history of philosophy.* Retrieved from the Internet March 21, 2003.

History of Copts. (2003) Coptic Digest Retrieved Jan 18, 2004 from
http://www.copts.netindex/asp

Janet,P. (1920) Major symptoms of hysteria. New York: McMillan Press

Keyes, D. (1981). The minds of billy milligan. New York: Bantam Books. Random

House

Langer, E. (1998) *PTSD: a diagnostic report on war veterans. Retrieved November 10, 2003 from*
http://www.geocities.com/southbeach/shores-/6052/ptsd.1.html

Masterson, J. (1990). The search for the real self. London: The Free Press.

McHugh, P. (2001). Retrieved April 3, 2004 from http://www.md.phy.com.net.mchugh.html.

Meyers,C. (1940). Shell Shock in France 1914-1918. Cambridge, MA: Cambridge United Press

Morris, A. (1989). Multiple personality disorder – an exercise in deception. Mahwah: Lawrence Earlbam and Associates. U.K.

Noll, A. (2002, November 31). Not the first OSU serial rapist. *The Lantern Newspaper.* Retrieved June 8, 2004 from http://www.thelantern.com/news/2002/10/31/Campus/Not-The.First.Osu.Serial.Rapist-31

Plato (1957). The republic. Oxford: Oxford

Press.

Pratnicka, W. (2004) Possessed by Ghosts – exorcisms in the twentieth century. Retrieved November 1, 2004 from http://www.theexorcisms.com/

Prince, M. (1906). The dissociation of a personality – classics in psychology. New York, NY: Longmans Press.

Putnam, F (1989). Diagnosis and treatment of multiple personality disorder. New York: Guilford Press.

Ross, C. (1989). Multiple personality disorder: diagnosis, clinical features, and treatment. New York: Wiley-Interscience. p.185.

Ross, C. (1989). Specific techniques of treating MPD. New York: John Wiley and Sons. 214-246.

Ross, C. (2000). Project bluebird. Richardson: Manitou Communications, Inc.

Salter W. (1961). *Zoar, or the evidence of psychological research concerning survival.*

Sidran Homepage. (2002). *Traumatic stress instruments and measures from sidran.* retrieved March 27, 2003 from http://www.sidran.org/dis.html.

Van Bergen, L. (1999) Zacht en eervol: lijden en striven in een grote oorlog. Nijmegen: SUA

Van Der Hart, O. (2000). Somatoform dissociation in traumatized world war I combat soldiers. A neglected clinical history. Journal of Trauma and Dissociation, 2000-1-(4), 38-66.

Witztum, E. (2004) *Language of science. How history affects the appraisal of psychological war casualties-obstacles to assessment of PTSD in longitudinal research.* retrieved June 28, 2004 from http://www.wkap.n//prod/b/o-306-46095-5?=a.html

Wozniak, Robert. (1906) *Morton prince dissociation of a personality 1906. Historical essay.* Retrieved March 1, 2004, from http://www.thoemmes.com/psych/prince/html